Thank you...

... for purchasing this copy of Get Ready for Year 1.

We hope that you will find this book helpful in preparing your child to move up to their next year-group. You may choose to use it during the final few months of Reception, during the summer holidays or in the first few months of Year 1.

On our Teachers and Parents pages we summarise the likely content of each subject in Year 1. On the children's pages we feature activities that will help prepare children for most of their subjects, hopefully giving them confidence to take part in their lessons with enthusiasm, skills and knowledge.

This book is part of our growing range of educational titles. Most of our books are individual workbooks but, due to popular demand, we are now introducing a greater number of photocopiable titles for teachers.

To find details of our other publications, please visit our website:

www.acblack.com

CONTENTS

During Year 1 the children will take part in a daily 'Numeracy Hour'. This starts with a whole class activity in which the children will practise number skills. The children then move to group activities - one group will work with the teacher while other groups work with a classroom assistant or without direct adult help. Towards the end of the lesson the teacher will bring the whole class together again for a 'plenary' in which the lesson's activities are discussed - this can be a very important time for reinforcing new concepts.

The work in Year 1 will include learning to:

✓ count objects, at least 20, without making mistakes;

✓ count on from any number less than 10;

✓ count back from any number less than 20;

✓ count on in tens, starting at zero;

✓ count back in tens, starting at one hundred;

✓ read and write all numbers up to 20 and be able to write these numbers in order;

✓ using numbers between 0 and 30, be able to say which number is 1 more or 1 less or 10 more or 10 less;

✓ understand simple additions and subtractions;

✓ know all the pairs of numbers that add up to 10;

✓ solve simple problems by using appropriate number skills;

✓ compare two objects by considering their lengths or their masses or their capacities;

✓ complete simple measurements of lengths, masses or capacities;

✓ describe simple shapes;

✓ read the time on a clock, to the hour or half hour;

✓ know a wide range of vocabulary involving time, including days of the week and seasons.

We suggest that you work through the following twelve pages with your child. Give her/him plenty of praise for success. If any page is too difficult at this stage, leave it for now and come back to it later. It is very important that children feel confident, even when they make mistakes or find some questions difficult.

BASIC SHAPES

Colour the circles red.

Colour the squares blue and the triangles yellow.

red circles
blue squares
yellow triangles

How many circles are there?

How many squares are there?

How many triangles are there?

MATCHING NUMBERS AND WORDS (1)

Here are the words.

four

one

six

three

two

five

Here are the numbers.

2

4

3

6

1

5

Write the numbers and words.
The first one is done for you.

•	1	one
••		
•••		
••••		
•••••		
••••••		

MATCHING WORDS AND NUMBERS (2)

Here are the words.

twelve

nine

seven

eleven

ten

eight

Here are the numbers.

8

10

11

12

7

9

Write the numbers and the words.

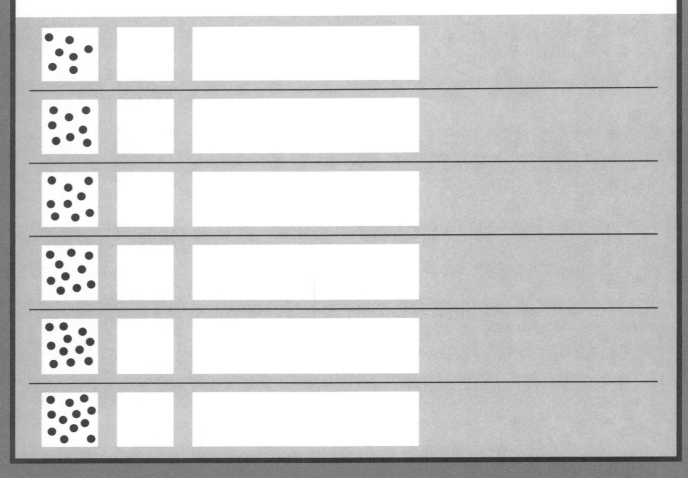

ADDITION

One add two makes three.

Two add one makes three.

Fill in the missing numbers.

$1 + 2 = 3$

$2 + 1 = 3$

$1 + 3 = 4$

$\quad + \quad = 4$

$\quad + \quad =$

$\quad + \quad =$

$\quad + \quad =$

$\quad + \quad =$

$\quad + \quad =$

$\quad + \quad =$

$\quad + \quad =$

$\quad + \quad =$

$\quad + \quad =$

$\quad + \quad =$

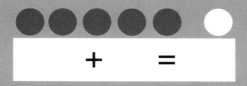

$\quad + \quad =$

Fill in the missing numbers.

$1 + 9 = 10$

$2 + 8 = 10$

$3 + 7 = $ _____

_____ $+$ _____ $= 10$

_____ $+$ _____ $= 10$

_____ $+$ _____ $=$

$7 + 3 = $ _____

$8 + 2 = $ _____

$9 + $ _____ $= 10$

$10 + 0 = $ _____

We need to know all these.

$0 + 10 = 10$ $6 + 4 = 10$
$1 + 9 = 10$ $7 + 3 = 10$
$2 + 8 = 10$ $8 + 2 = 10$
$3 + 7 = 10$ $9 + 1 = 10$
$4 + 6 = 10$ $10 + 0 = 10$
$5 + 5 = 10$

TIME (1)

This clock shows...

9 o'clock

What time do these clocks show?

TIME (2)

Match the clocks to the correct times.

The first one is done for you.

Half past five.

Half past three.

Half past eight.

Half past twelve.

Half past two.

Half past ten.

THERE ARE 7 DAYS IN 1 WEEK

Copy the name of each day.

Draw a picture of yourself as you are dressed today.

Monday

Tuesday

Wednesday

Thursday

Friday

Saturday

Sunday

THERE ARE 7 DAYS IN 1 WEEK

Answer these questions about days.

What day is it today?

What day was it yesterday?

What day will it be tomorrow?

On what days do you go to school?

Draw a picture to show what the weather is like today.

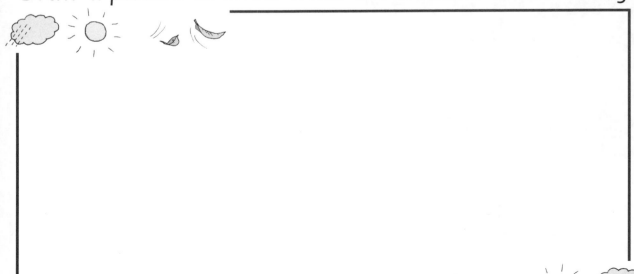

SUBTRACTION (1)

Notes for adults. Subtraction can be difficult for children as it concerns two different concepts: 'take away' and 'find the difference'. On this page we are dealing with taking away. We show a picture of several circles and ask the children to take some away but, as they cannot be removed from the page, we suggest that you encourage the children to draw crosses on the ones to be taken away, then count how many are uncrossed. Alternatively you could use counters, buttons, shells, etc., to represent the circles, then physically take away the appropriate number. We have completed the first question as an example.

$6 - 2 = \boxed{4}$

$5 - 3 = \boxed{}$

$7 - 1 = \boxed{}$

$7 - 2 = \boxed{}$

$9 - 3 = \boxed{}$

$9 - 4 = \boxed{}$

$7 - 5 = \boxed{}$

$8 - 2 = \boxed{}$

$10 - 4 = \boxed{}$

$10 - 2 = \boxed{}$

ADDING USING A NUMBER LINE

You can use a number line to help you when you add.

Look: 6 + 4

Start at the number 6.

Make 4 jumps forward.

6 + 4 = 10

Use this number line to help you to answer these questions.

2 + 3 =	5 + 4 =	6 + 3 =
4 + 4 =	8 + 4 =	3 + 6 =
5 + 2 =	9 + 5 =	11 + 2 =
13 + 4 =	15 + 1 =	12 + 3 =
14 + 6 =	18 + 1 =	19 + 1 =

SUBTRACTION (2)

Note for adults. Please see the notes on page 13. On this page we are looking at 'finding the difference' and we use a number line to show this. The first question provides an example to show how to do the others. It is a good idea to show the children that we 'make two jumps' to get from 6 <u>back</u> to 4.

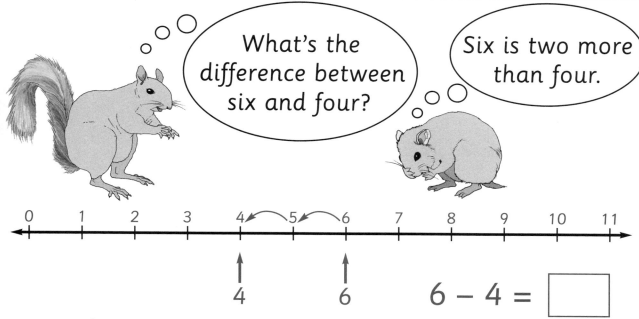

6 − 4 = ☐

Use the number line to help you to answer these questions.

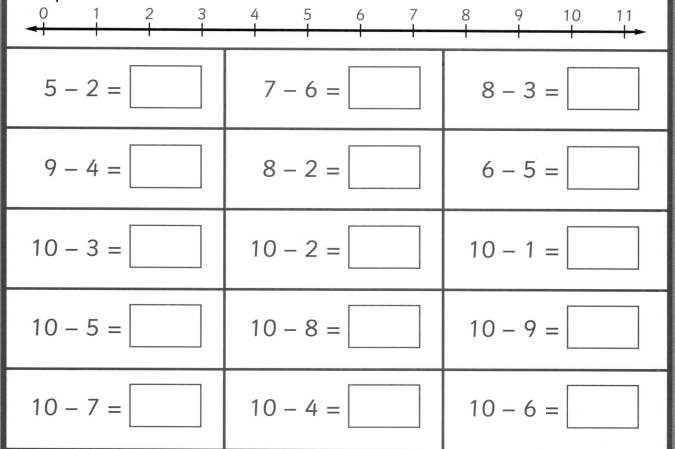

5 − 2 = ☐	7 − 6 = ☐	8 − 3 = ☐
9 − 4 = ☐	8 − 2 = ☐	6 − 5 = ☐
10 − 3 = ☐	10 − 2 = ☐	10 − 1 = ☐
10 − 5 = ☐	10 − 8 = ☐	10 − 9 = ☐
10 − 7 = ☐	10 − 4 = ☐	10 − 6 = ☐

During their literacy work in Year 1, your children will build on the work they have done in Reception. They will experience the daily literacy lesson, in which they will read books guided by their teachers and will learn about aspects of spelling, grammar and writing. The lessons will include work on:

✓   Correct letter formation;

✓   Developing a comfortable and efficient pencil grip;

✓   Alphabetical order;

✓   Developing simple phonic skills;

✓   Recognition of high frequency words;

✓   Capital letters and full stops;

✓   Rhyming words;

✓   Reading comprehension;

✓   Words ending in ff, ll, ss, ck, ng;

✓   Words with oo, ee, ai, ie, oa;

✓   Word order within sentences;

✓   Vowels and consonants;

✓   Making simple story books;

✓   Reading and following simple instructions;

✓   Writing simple questions.

Introductory work for many of the above points will be found in the literacy pages in this book.

ALPHABETICAL ORDER

The alphabet is always written in the same order.

a b c d e f g h i j k l m n o p q r s t u v w x y z

Fill in the missing letters below.

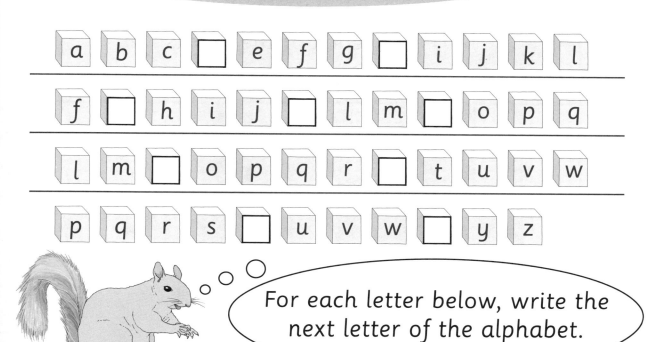

a b c ☐ e f g ☐ i j k l

f ☐ h i j ☐ l m ☐ o p q

l m ☐ o p q r ☐ t u v w

p q r s ☐ u v w ☐ y z

For each letter below, write the next letter of the alphabet.

I have done the first one for you.

a b	n	r	e
t	l	s	y
v	b	u	j
o	d	h	q

VOWELS

The letters **a**, **e**, **i**, **o** and **u** are called **vowels**.
They are important as there is a vowel in nearly every word.

Use the picture clues to help you to put the missing vowel in each of the words.

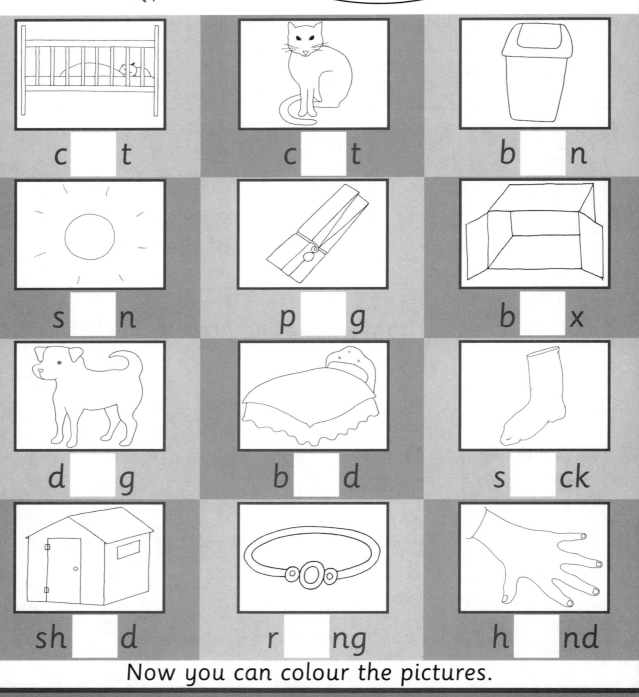

c ☐ t

c ☐ t

b ☐ n

s ☐ n

p ☐ g

b ☐ x

d ☐ g

b ☐ d

s ☐ ck

sh ☐ d

r ☐ ng

h ☐ nd

Now you can colour the pictures.

HANDWRITING

a b c d e f g h i j k l m n o p q r s t u v w x y z

All the letters written in black are letters that start the same way when you write them.

Practise writing the letter c. Always start it at the top.

c c c c

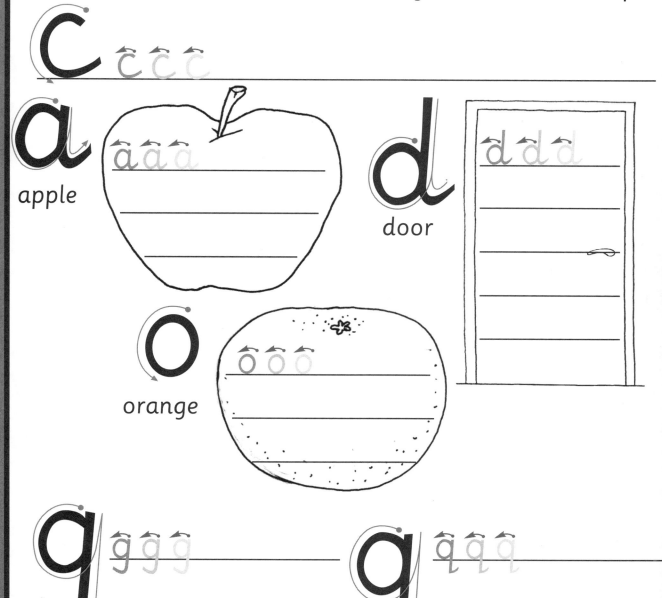

a a a a

apple

d d d d

door

o o o o

orange

g g g g

q q q q

MUDDLED SENTENCES

My sentences are in a muddle.

Can you write them correctly?

The capital letters and the full stops will help you.

going I swimming. am

_____

called Sally. My sister is

_____

I night. to go at bed

_____

in water is river. the There

_____

game. a I play want to

_____

dog The for went a walk.

_____

'OO' AND 'EE'

Put **ee** or **oo** in the words below.
The picture clues will help you.

sh __ __ p

m __ __ n

tr __ __

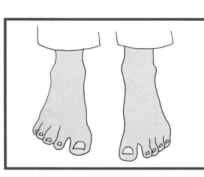

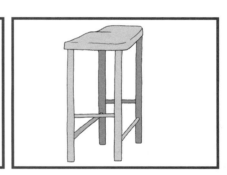

b __ __ t

f __ __ t

st __ __ l

Now find the words in the word search and colour them yellow.

```
s h e e p w x z r w q l
n o n r s t o o l w s r
l l e r s d f e r d p p
b o r b o o t e d o v f
n t r e e w t q f e e t
m o o n w o o e e s d r
```

Write over each of these letters.
They all start from the top.

Now practice writing them inside the pictures.

umbrella

mouse

rabbit

nest

Carefully read and write each of the words below.

nod	run	gum	drum
_____	_____	_____	_____
mud	man	moon	good
_____	_____	_____	_____

COMPREHENSION (1)

You must read the writing carefully to be able to finish the picture and colour it correctly.

The house has two windows, a green door and a brown roof with a chimney. The sky is blue and a big yellow sun is shining brightly. An orange car is next to the house. There is an apple tree in the garden. It has four red apples and two green ones growing on it. Some yellow flowers are growing near the garden gate.

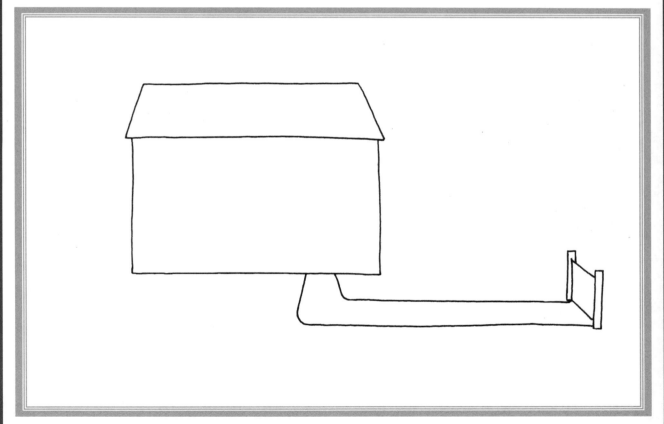

Now draw yourself in the picture.

Practice writing the letters s and l on the lines below.

Read the words, and write them in the correct boxes.

mess	bell	miss	less
tell	fall	kiss	dress
pull	wall	fuss	mill

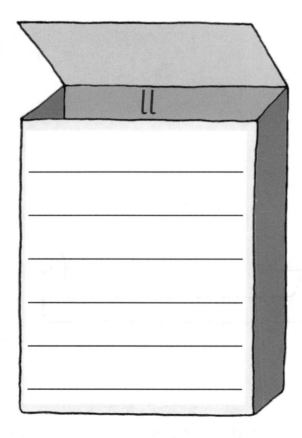

ll

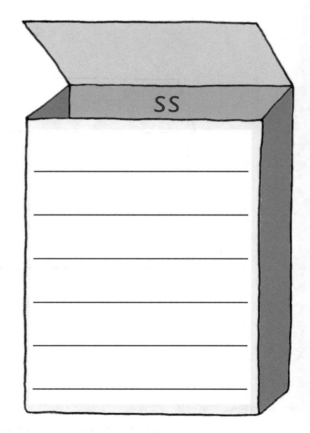

ss

WORD JIGSAWS

My words have been cut in two.

Join them up and label the pictures.

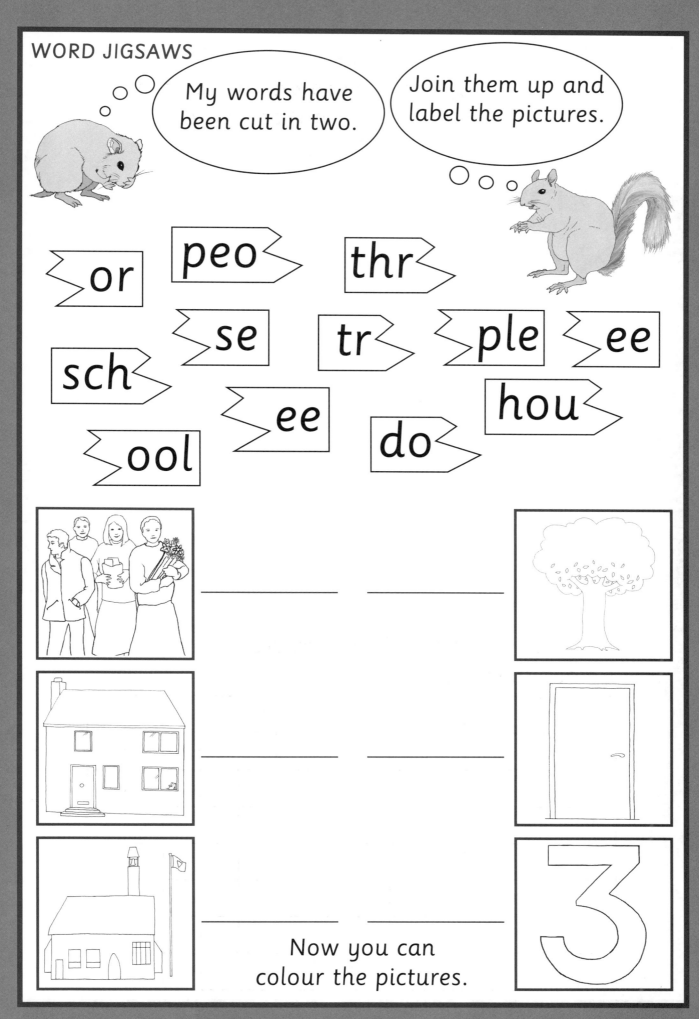

or

peo

thr

se

tr

ple

ee

sch

ee

hou

ool

do

Now you can colour the pictures.

HIGH FREQUENCY WORDS

Read and write each of these words.

because	said	when
_____	_____	_____

next	night	about
_____	_____	_____

once	school	laugh
_____	_____	_____

would	should	were
_____	_____	_____

Find the words in this wordsearch.
Colour them yellow.

a	b	b	e	c	a	u	s	e	w	q	e	r	a
s	h	o	u	l	d	x	r	t	s	a	i	d	v
e	r	t	s	c	h	o	o	l	t	w	e	r	e
y	t	h	w	o	u	l	d	w	o	t	z	t	r
n	e	x	t	o	n	g	t	d	e	o	n	c	e
w	h	e	n	s	a	b	o	u	t	e	r	l	p
t	r	e	u	w	l	a	u	g	h	h	v	t	u	l
b	e	w	r	n	i	g	h	t	s	d	p	l	o

RHYMING WORDS

Choose a word from the pin board to rhyme with each pair of words.
Write it in the box.

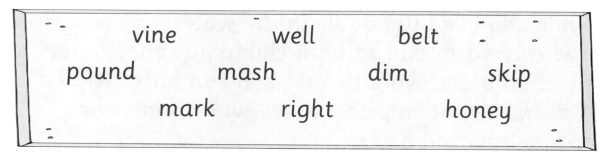

vine   well   belt

pound   mash   dim   skip

mark   right   honey

chip
flip)

bell
fell)

mine
fine)

splash
flash)

money
funny)

felt
melt)

park
shark)

gym
trim)

found
ground)

night
light)

Handwriting
Carefully copy these letters.

COMPREHENSION (2)

Read this carefully.

Jack and Lily were going to the beach for the day. They were excited. Jack loved to build sandcastles, while Lily liked to paddle in the water.

It was a warm day so both children rubbed in lots of sun cream and wore t-shirts and sun hats. At one o'clock they ate a picnic lunch with sandwiches, crisps, fruit and drink.

At five o'clock the two tired children were taken home.

They had enjoyed a lovely day out.

What were the children called?	Zak and Tilly	☐
	Jack and Lily	☐
	Max and Milly	☐

What did Lily like to do?	Paddle in the water	☐
	Swim in the sea	☐
	Build sandcastles	☐

When did the children go home?	One o'clock	☐
	Three o'clock	☐
	Five o'clock	☐

In the box, draw a sandcastle with a green and red flag on top.

The National curriculum shows that every child in Year 1 needs to be taught Science and the 'foundation subjects', Art, Design Technology, Geography, History, Information Technology, Music and Physical Education, together with Religious Education.

✓   SCIENCE

In Year 1, the children will learn about several aspects of science:

'Ourselves' - learning about parts of the body and about smell, hearing, sight and taste.

Growing - particularly the growth of plants.

Materials - sorting objects by their properties (rough, smooth, hard, soft, etc.) and by the names of materials (wood, metal, glass, plastic, etc.)

Light and Dark - naming sources of light, including the Sun, learning that it is dangerous to look at the Sun.

Movement - observing that movement can be caused by pushing or pulling something.

Sound - recognising many sounds, making comparisons and realising that they hear sounds through their ears.

✓   DT

During Year 1 the children begin to develop an understanding of Design Technology by creating a simple picture with moving parts. They observe a range of playground equipment and make models of items such as swings and climbing frames. Similarly, they will gain understanding of structures by observing homes and making a model home that includes windows and doors. In considering food technology the children will learn about a variety of fruit and vegetables and may have the opportunity to make a food product by cutting and combining them.

✓   IT

Many children will have experience of using computers at home and they will extend this in school by:

➤ using the mouse to select pictures and text, matching them on screen;

➤ using a simple word processor, learning appropriate technical vocabulary such as delete, enter, key, keyboard, print, printer, select and space bar;

➤ using key words from a word bank to label pictures on the screen;

➤ entering simple information into a graphing program and observing the pictograms created;

➤ learning about providing appropriate instructions, perhaps by using a robot which moves on the floor.

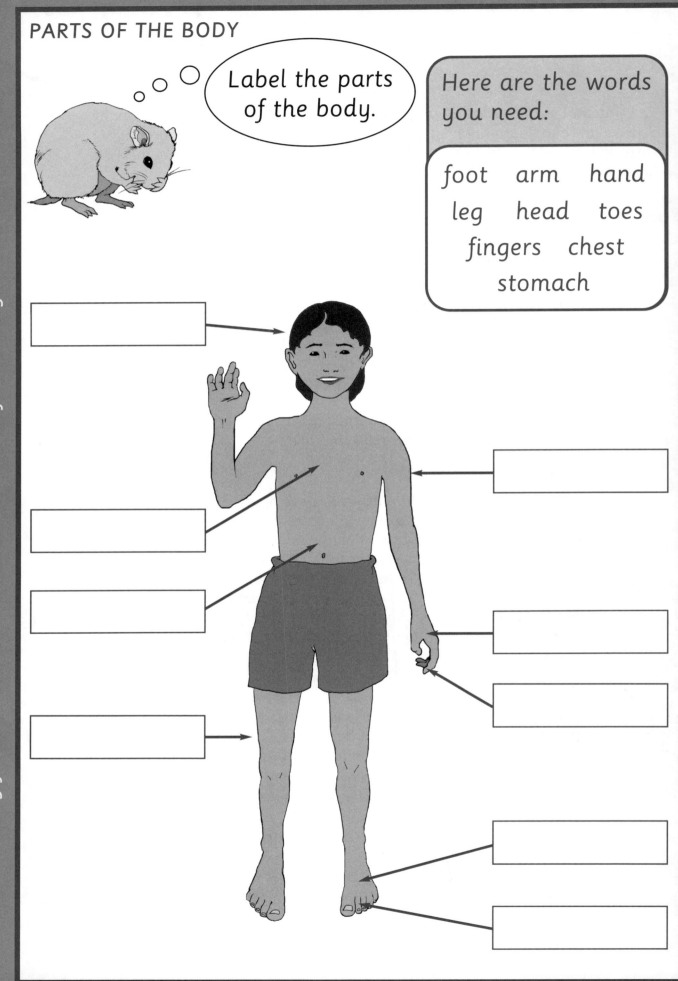

Label the parts of the body.

Here are the words you need:

foot   arm   hand
leg   head   toes
fingers   chest
stomach

PARTS OF THE HEAD

We use our eyes to see with.

We use our nose to smell with.

What do we use our ears for?

Label the face: ear, mouth, eye, nose, chin

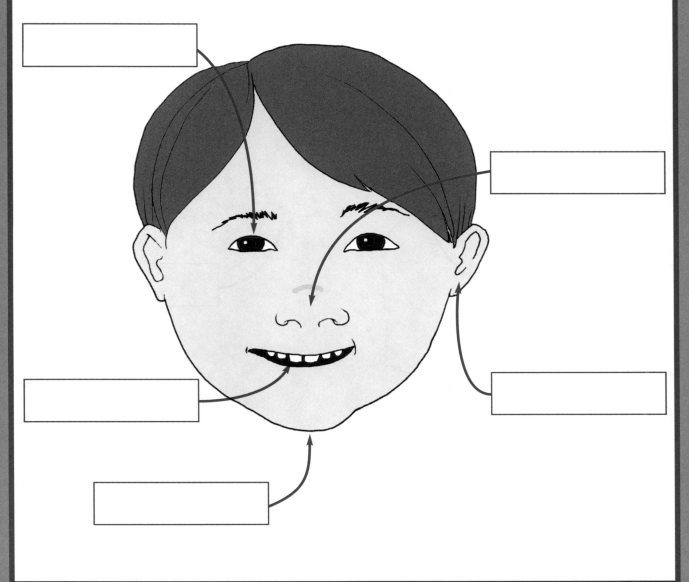

PARTS OF A TREE

Label the tree.

Here are the words:

leaf   root   trunk
branch

Colour the tree carefully.

FRUIT AND VEGETABLES

I like fruit.

I like vegetables.

carrot

apple

orange

peas

pepper

banana

Colour the fruit and vegetables.
Write the words in the correct basket.

FRUIT

VEGETABLES

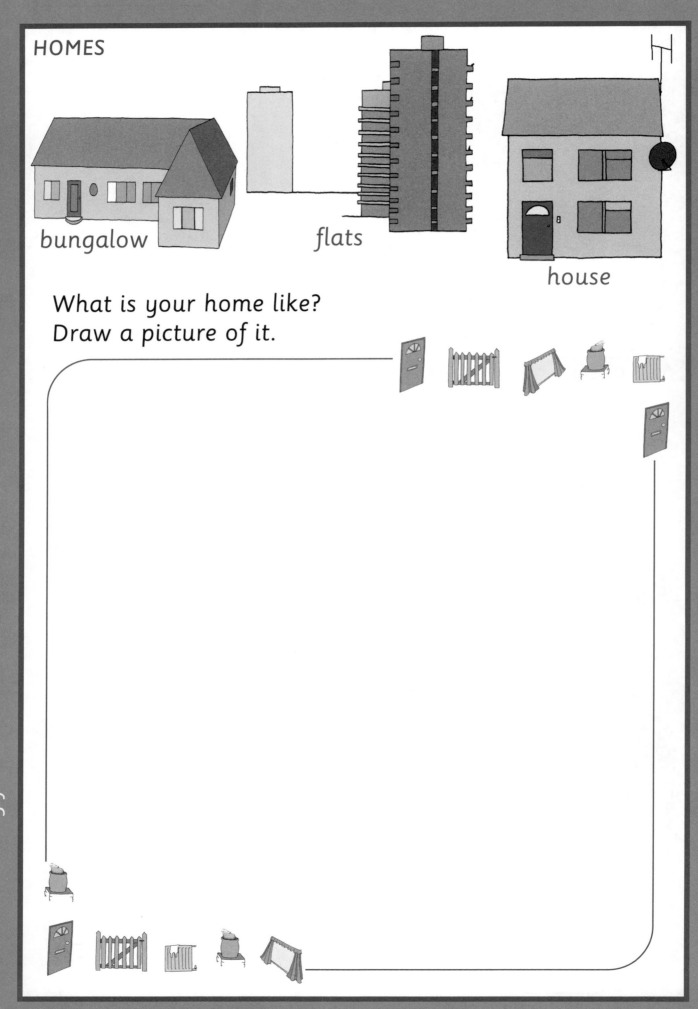

bungalow

flats

house

What is your home like?
Draw a picture of it.

✓ MUSIC
Music is very much a practical subject, and during the year pupils are likely to use simple percussion instruments quite regularly. They will be taught to use these instruments correctly and to be able to name them. They will also develop their performing skills through using their voices. There will be opportunities to develop their listening skills throughout the year, and there will be an emphasis on recognising rhythms and long and short sounds. In this book we have included work on identifying a range of musical instruments.

✓ RE
During Year 1, children are likely to study what 'belonging' means and what it means to belong to a particular religion. They will consider beliefs and practices, why Christians give gifts at Christmas and how we can learn from visiting a church.

✓ HISTORY
In Year 1 children are likely to cover work on how our toys today differ from those used in the past, and what homes were like a long time ago. They may also do a topic on what seaside holidays were like in the past. In this book we have included work on aspects of homes in the present and past.

✓ GEOGRAPHY
During Year 1 the children will study the local area close to the school. They will learn to use appropriate vocabulary, such as the names of buildings. As an aspect of this, the children will be asked to write out their home address and to discuss what each line of the address means. They will look at simple maps and pictures of the area and will work with the teacher to follow directions. They will also consider how to make the local area safer, perhaps considering a particular issue such as parking.

✓ ART
During Year 1 or Year 2, children will draw a self-portrait. They will use a variety of materials for drawing and painting, such as pencils, charcoal, crayons, block paints, powder paints and liquid paints. They will have opportunities to work with textiles, for example in weaving and collage. They will examine sculptures and produce their own three-dimensional work. They are likely to produce photographs using a digital camera. They will observe the shapes and patterns on buildings.

✓ PHYSICAL EDUCATION
The children are likely to take part in:
➙ Games, practising basic skills such as throwing and catching;
➙ Dance, using different parts of their bodies to vary their movements in jumping, turning, spinning, and hopping. They will be encouraged to consider the culture and history behind different dances. Working with a partner will be an important aspect of dance and other PE activities;
➙ Gymnastics, working on the floor or on apparatus. The children will be taught to make good use of space, avoiding each other for safety;
➙ Swimming will not take place in all schools, as some prefer to wait until Year 2 or Year 3. The emphasis will be to encourage confidence through learning how to keep afloat and to move in the water, at first with the use of a swimming aid if needed.

NEW AND OLD HOMES

Some of the objects below belong in the very old house and some belong in the new one.

Write the names in the correct house box below.
You may want to try to draw the pictures too.

candle

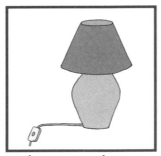
electric lamp

sink

washstand

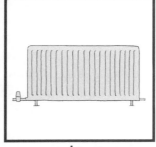
radiator

fireplace

doorbell

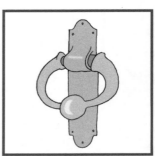
door knocker

OLD HOUSE

NEW HOUSE
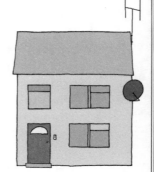

CHURCHES

Have you ever visited a church?
Here are some of the things you might find in a church.
Write the correct name under each picture.

Bible   candles   stained glass window   font

_____   _____

_____

_____

_____

Now colour the stained glass window.

MUSICAL INSTRUMENTS

Name the instruments and colour them.

Choose the names from the box.

xylophone   maracas   claves

triangle   guitar

cymbals   drums   saxophone

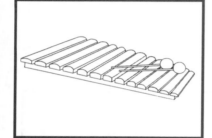

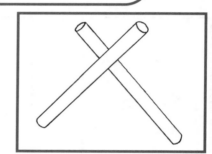

_____   _____   _____

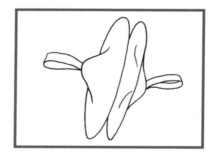

_____   _____

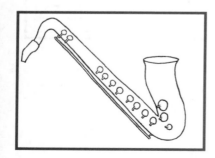

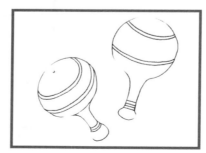

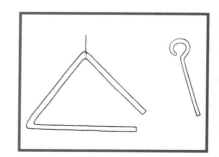

_____   _____   _____

YOUR ADDRESS

Notes for adults: During Year 1, the children are likely to be asked to write their address. This is a very difficult activity for most children of this age so this page provides an excellent opportunity to practise. We suggest that you write the address clearly on a separate piece of paper for your child to copy. Discuss what each line means and try to encourage your child to copy each line completely, rather than spilling over to the next line.

My address.

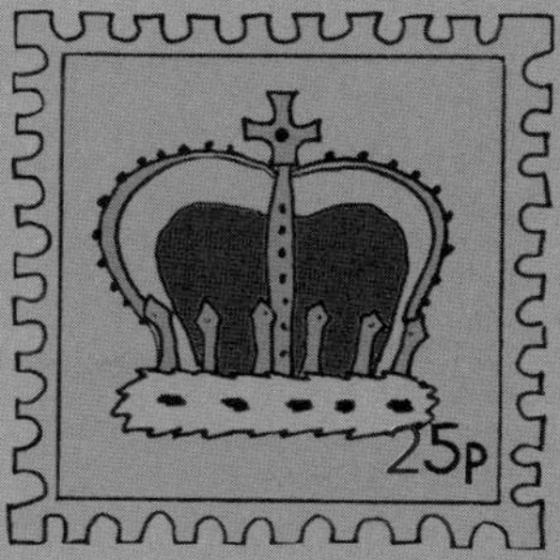

PICTURE MAP

Colour this picture map.

Sam's house

Kim's house

Arti's house

Who lives next door to Sam?

Who lives next door to Arti?